DERBYSHIRE MURDER STORIES

RECALLING THE EVENTS OF SOME OF DERBYSHIRE'S MOST WELL KNOWN MURDERS

David J A Bell

BRADWELL
BOOKS

Published by Bradwell Books

9 Orgreave Close Sheffield S13 9NP

Email: books@bradwellbooks.co.uk

British Library Cataloguing in Publication Data: a catalogue record for this book is available from the British Library.

1st Edition

ISBN: 9781909914285

Print: Gomer Press, Llandysul, Ceredigion SA44 4JL

Design by: Andrew Caffrey
Typesetting by: Mark Titterton

Photograph Credits: Photography by the Author
unless otherwise stated

CONTENTS

INTRODUCTION

In this book of Derbyshire murders, the stories range from 1758 to 1978. In 1758, two young lovers, eloping to be married at Derbyshire's own Gretna Green, were murdered for their money by four local men in the bleak Winnats Pass. In 1821, a duel took place in Winster between a retired naval surgeon and the son of a solicitor, who disapproved of the doctor's affection for his sister. The doctor was fatally wounded – but was only one of the pistols loaded?

Following the murder of a woman in 1973, a young Bakewell man was found guilty of the crime. When the editor of a Derbyshire newspaper took up his claim that he was innocent, the investigation made international headlines. The conviction was eventually found to be unsafe and the man was released after having been in prison for 27 years. If he had not continued to claim his innocence throughout his prison sentence, he would have been released ten years earlier.

Also included is a case where the son of a vicar shot dead a policeman during a wild escapade, and the killing of a strange travelling conjuror nicknamed Mexican Joe. There is also the account of how a courageous Derby grandmother fought for eighteen years to bring the murderer of her granddaughter to justice. She was eventually successful in her quest.

Add in the murders of a Repton baker, and a young lady who had changed her mind about her engagement, plus the death of Knocky Stone, a much-respected Spondon man, and the reader will find much of interest in the crimes that have occurred in the county of Derbyshire.

David J. A. Bell

Winnats Pass in winter
(Mark Titterton)

THE MURDER OF KNOCKY STONE

ENOCH 'KNOCKY' STONE LIVED IN CHURCH STREET, SPONDON, WITH HIS TWO DAUGHTERS. HE HAD A SON IN SERVICE IN DERBY, AND KNOCKY WOULD COLLECT HIS SON'S CLOTHES AND TAKE THEM HOME TO WASH. HE WAS NOT A WEALTHY MAN, BEING A FRAMEWORK KNITTER BY TRADE. HE WAS A RELIGIOUS MAN, AND A REGULAR WORSHIPER AT ST WERBURGH'S CHURCH IN SPONDON. THE CHURCH ORGAN WAS, OF COURSE, POWERED BY AIR PRESSURE, AND IN THOSE DAYS SOMEONE HAD TO MANUALLY PUMP THE AIR. AT SPONDON CHURCH, ENOCH STONE FULFILLED THAT ROLE FOR ALL SERVICES, WEDDINGS AND OTHER EVENTS. HE WAS SMALL IN STATURE, AND WAS DISABLED WITH A FORM OF PARTIAL PARALYSIS WHICH CAUSED HIM TO WALK WITH A PRONOUNCED LIMP.

This simple monument marks the spot where Enoch Stone was murdered

On Monday 23rd June 1856, after his daughters had come home from work at 8pm, the 49-year-old Knocky set out to walk the four miles into Derby to collect his son's washing. With his hobbling gait, this must have taken him some time. He then began the slow journey home, carrying a basket of his son's clothes. When he reached Chaddesden, he called in at the Plough Inn for a cheese sandwich and a drink, then set off again for Spondon. He'd had just one drink, and was perfectly sober.

However, he never reached his home. He was seen still limping along at 10.54pm, but shortly afterwards he was attacked, and left bleeding in the hedge. He had been beaten about the head with a blunt instrument, probably a tree branch, receiving several serious wounds, which bled profusely, and a fractured skull. As he lay groaning and bleeding in the hedge-bottom, he was seen by several passers-by, who took one look at him before deciding he was obviously drunk and continuing their journey.

It was two coachmen who proved to be Good Samaritans. At the junction of Nottingham Road and Oregon Way, they saw what they took to be a pile of rags at the side of the road, but on checking found that it was the severely injured Enoch Stone. The policeman from Spondon was sent for, and he fetched in the local doctor, James Cade. Knocky was carried on a cart to his home in Church

Street and Dr Cade stayed all night with him, but the injured man died at 6am on Tuesday morning without regaining consciousness.

The local community was outraged. Enoch had been a popular local resident and was highly regarded by everyone. It seems to have been a robbery, but he had been killed for very little. His killer or killers had emptied his pockets, but Knocky never had more than a few pennies on him. His boots had been stolen too, but they would not have been of much use to the thieves as they were of different sizes. Some of his son's clothing had been stolen from the basket, with the rest strewn around at the scene.

A few people were taken in for questioning by the police, including a tramp who was seen carrying a pair of boots, and two Irish navvies who had been seen in Chaddesden on the Monday evening. Perhaps the authorities were keen to prove that it was no one local who had committed this brutal crime. All three had alibis, however, and were released.

A week later, a poster offering a reward was issued. The authorities offered a £100 reward for any information that might lead to the apprehension of the culprits – a considerable sum in 1856. The residents of Spondon raised another £20 to add to it, proving yet again how loved Enoch Stone had been in the area. His inquest

was held at the Malt Shovel in Spondon on 21st July, before Sir Henry Wilmot, JP, of Chaddesden Hall, and a verdict was returned of 'murder by persons unknown'.

Although his killers were never caught, Knocky was not forgotten. A stone bearing the initials ES was placed at the scene of the murder, and although somewhat weather-worn, it is still there today. Just round the corner there is a street named Enoch Stone Drive. These two memorials indicate how much the local community missed the framework knitter from Spondon.

SON OF A VICAR

GERALD MAINWARING CAME FROM A RESPECTABLE AND WELL-TO-DO FAMILY WHO LIVED IN WHITFIELD HALL. HIS FATHER – THE REVD WILLIAM MAINWARING – WAS A CLERGYMAN AND A MAGISTRATE, AND HIS GRANDFATHER ROWLAND MAINWARING HAD BEEN AN ADMIRAL IN THE ROYAL NAVY. AN OLDER BROTHER BECAME A GENERAL IN THE ARMY. HOWEVER, GERALD, THE SIXTH OF EIGHT CHILDREN, HAD BEEN SENT TO RESIDE IN CANADA TO SOW HIS WILD OATS, AS HE HAD A PRODIGIOUS APPETITE FOR BOTH WOMEN AND ALCOHOL.

However, in April 1879 he was back in England to attend his sister's wedding. He was due to return to Manitoba in July, but he was determined to have a grand spree before he went. He chose the town of Derby for the enterprise.

On 10th July, he bought an ivory-handled revolver and five hundred cartridges in a shop run by a Mrs Dobson. He then booked into the Royal Hotel in Victoria Street, and spent the first day there drinking whisky and sherry

11

with a male friend. By the second day he had a local prostitute, Annie Green, living there with him. Gerald found Annie good company and a great drinking companion; she could match him drink for drink. They spent two whole days there, drinking champagne and brandy all day and all evening, but caused no trouble to the staff.

On Saturday 12th July, Annie and Gerald got through three pints of claret and a quart of brandy before going to visit the house where Annie lived and worked. He stated that he wanted to take Annie away for a few days. At first the request was refused, but when the inebriated Gerald produced the revolver and began clumsily to load it, permission was quickly granted.

The tipsy couple got back into the trap in which they'd arrived, Gerald taking the reins, and began a wild ride back through the streets of Derby. They were both laughing and cursing at the people they met. Annie was so merry that she was hanging out of the trap, which attracted the attention of the passers-by. A police officer, Constable Clamp, realised that the trap was being driven by someone under the influence of drink. He and other officers followed and managed to arrest Gerald Mainwaring and Annie Green in the yard of the Traveller's Rest on Ashbourne Road. The couple had stopped there as they were obviously in need of another drink!

The pair were taken to the police station in Lock-up Yard. The police were kept very busy by Annie, who was swearing and falling over by this stage. She was trying to fight them all, and certainly managed to punch at least one policeman on the chin. The police had not got round to searching Gerald, who had walked behind a screen, from where he suddenly produced his loaded revolver and shot a constable, PC Joseph Moss. Another constable, PC Bill Price, rushed at the armed man, who fired at him. The second shot went harmlessly through his helmet, though a third wounded him in the arm. Mainwaring was then overpowered. During the struggle a fourth shot was fired, but hit no one.

The two wounded constables were taken to the infirmary, where PC Price recovered. Unfortunately, PC Moss, a former soldier, died of his wound the following day. Back in Lock-up Yard, an inspector tried to interview Gerald, who was still full of drunken bravado. He refused to co-operate, laughingly giving his name as 'Jeremiah from Jerusalem'.

The trial of 23-year-old Mainwaring was held very rapidly by the standards of today. He had killed PC Moss on 12th July and his trial began on 31st July, just nineteen days later. Gerald's wealthy family had hired the services of the solicitor general to defend their wayward son. The only point of contention for the jury to consider was whether there was malicious intent

IN MEMORY OF PC 35 JOSEPH MOSS

AGED 26 YEARS OF DERBY BOROUGH POLICE FORCE

FORMERLY OF THE GRENADIER GUARDS

WHO WAS MURDERED HERE ON 12TH JULY 1879

IN THE EXECUTION OF HIS DUTY

The plaque in Derby's fish market,
an area formerly known as Lock-up Yard

when the shots were fired. The solicitor general argued
that Gerald Mainwaring had been so 'wretchedly and
hopelessly drunk' at the time that he had no malice
towards PC Moss, who had not even spoken to him.
The prosecution countered by saying that drunkenness
could not be allowed to reduce the charge as this would
open the door to any future killer claiming that he was
drunk at the time.

The jury retired but could not agree. They divided six-six on whether the verdict should be murder or manslaughter. After a short discussion, they decided that the fairest way to make their choice was by tossing a coin! In this way, a man's life was to be decided. Heads would mean murder and the death sentence, while tails would mean manslaughter and imprisonment. It came down heads, and they brought in a verdict of murder. They did add a recommendation for mercy, perhaps feeling embarrassed about the use of a toss of a coin to decide if a man was to be hanged or not. The judge ignored the recommendation and Gerald Mainwaring was sentenced to death.

However, one of the jury talked, and when it became known that his fate had been left to a toss of a coin, there was a public outcry. The influential Mainwaring family had many friends in high places, and eventually their campaign was successful. The death sentence was revoked and the vicar's son was sent to prison. He served his sentence in Chatham prison, and went back to Canada after his release.

A plaque recording the death of PC Joseph Moss is to be found in Derby's fish market, which occupies the site of the former Lock-up Yard.

THE BAKEWELL CEMETERY MURDER

THE CASE OF THE MURDER OF 33-YEAR-OLD WENDY SEWELL ON WEDNESDAY 12TH SEPTEMBER 1973 BECAME INTERNATIONALLY NOTORIOUS AS AN EXAMPLE OF A MISCARRIAGE OF JUSTICE. IN THE CEMETERY IN BAKEWELL, SHE WAS FATALLY STRUCK ABOUT THE HEAD AND SHOULDERS SIX OR SEVEN TIMES WITH A PICKAXE HANDLE. THE YOUTH WHO DISCOVERED THE INJURED WOMAN WAS 17-YEAR-OLD STEPHEN DOWNING, WHO WORKED THERE.

Stephen was not very bright, and when he left school at 16 he had a reading age of only 11. He lived with his parents, Ray and Nita, on a local council estate, where he was known as a kind and caring boy, always willing to help people. The consensus on the estate was that he was 'a bit daft', but passive and gentle. His only real fault was that he could be rather lazy, and found it hard to get out of bed in the mornings. His first job after school was at Bloomers the bakers in the town centre. He caused a lot of amusement there when he created rather unusual gingerbread men and women. Let's just say that it was obvious which were which. Most people in Bakewell found this funny, and his employers still displayed his creations in the shop window. However, this trivial incident did lead to him being wrongly described later by a police officer as 'a known pervert'.

It was not his gingerbread creations that led to him getting the sack, but his poor timekeeping. He then found work with the local council as a gardener in the town cemetery. On the day of the murder, he had got up late and rushed to work, only to realise that he had put on his shoes rather than his work boots. He nipped home at 1pm to change his footwear, and asked his mum to buy him a bottle of pop and bring it down to the cemetery for him. When he got back to the cemetery, he found the badly injured Wendy Sewell lying on the cemetery footpath. Stephen knelt down and turned her over. She was still alive and tried to sit up, splattering him with drops of blood. The boy ran to the lodge to find his boss, Wilf Walker. The two of them returned to the path. Wendy had somehow managed to walk or crawl some yards but had fallen against a gravestone. Four workmen came over to see what was happening. The police and an ambulance were sent for.

Bakewell
(Mark Titterton)

A police constable arrived and took charge of the situation. He told everyone not to touch anything, and Stephen told him that he had turned her over when he found her. PC Ball told Stephen that he was not to wash the blood off his hands, but did allow the boy to carry on with his work, loading some asbestos into a van. A bloodstained pickaxe shaft was found nearby, and Stephen told the policeman that it must have come from the store in the disused chapel.

Forty minutes after Stephen had found the injured Wendy Sewell, the ambulance arrived and took her to Chesterfield Royal Hospital. There she was found to have multiple fractures of the skull. The police took Stephen Downing to the police station to be interviewed, and he was questioned virtually non-stop for nine hours. He was not allowed to see his family or a solicitor, and at times they had to shake him to keep him awake. By the end of this period, he was tired, hungry and very frightened. He was also suffering from an abscess on his back, which was causing him discomfort. The police kept alleging that he had assaulted Wendy Sewell before going home to change his shoes, returning to the cemetery and pretending to find her. They said they would keep questioning him all night if necessary. Eventually, at 10.30pm he was cautioned, and half an hour later he agreed to sign a confession. The police wrote out the statement, supposedly from his spoken words, but the confession uses phrases and vocabulary that were unlikely to be those of a youth with a reading age of 11. The confession was written in pencil, although he was asked to sign it with a ballpoint pen.

Later he was to explain that he thought the lady would tell the police that it wasn't him when she recovered, and he could then withdraw the false confession. However, Wendy Sewell died two days later. Although the confession written by the police and signed by Stephen Downing stated that he had hit her twice, a post-mortem established that she had been hit six or seven times in a frenzied attack. The police had not had the benefit of the pathologist's findings when they were writing out Stephen's confession. Thirteen days later, Stephen Downing retracted the confession, saying that it was untrue.

At the trial, which was now a murder trial, a witness stated that she had seen a tall, fair-haired man running away from the cemetery area at 1.15pm on the day of the murder. However, the trial put much more emphasis on Stephen's signed confession, and he was found guilty. As he was under eighteen his sentence was that he should be detained 'at Her Majesty's Pleasure', with a recommendation that he should serve seventeen years.

An appeal was heard eight months later. At this, a fifteen-year-old girl gave evidence that she had seen Wendy Sewell and a man with their arms around each other on the day Wendy was attacked. Wendy was known to have enjoyed an active and varied love life. The girl's evidence was judged unreliable because she had not come forward at the time of the trial, although she explained that she had been afraid the man might come after her if she had done so.

Stephen was not released after seventeen years. The main factor that kept him in prison was that he still claimed to be innocent of the crime. If he had said he had done it, he would have been set free, but his denial kept him inside. Although everyone at his prison found him polite and co-operative to both staff and inmates, and 'his attitude towards women has been commendable', his release was always refused on the ground that he was in denial of guilt. This meant that, despite being categorised as being no danger to the public, Stephen could not be considered for release while he continued to say that he had not committed the murder of Wendy Sewell.

He had been in prison for twenty years when a courageous local newspaper editor took up his case. Don Hale, editor of the Matlock Mercury, gradually became convinced that further investigation into the case was required. As he ran his campaign, Don Hale needed all his strength of will and physical courage, and suffered three attempts on his own life. He discovered that Wendy had had affairs with a number of prominent local businessmen and farmers. He found that one of her ex-lovers had concocted a false alibi for himself, but had been seen in Bakewell that day. He discovered that Wendy had been visited by a man at her place of work at about 12.25pm on the day of her murder. Three young children told him that they had been terrified when a bloodstained man had leapt over the cemetery wall where they were playing on the day in question. Other witnesses spoke of seeing a man in an orange T-shirt hanging about the cemetery just before the attack. Everyone who reported their evidence to the police said that they had not been taken seriously, being told that 'we've already got someone in custody'.

Don Hale's investigations met a continual stone wall of silence from the authorities. He was astounded to be told that all the papers connected with the case, and the bloodstained murder weapon, had been destroyed. The official silence contrasted with the many ordinary Bakewell people who told him that they had always believed that the convicted young gardener was not guilty. Don's campaign to get the case looked at again lasted seven years. Eventually, the appeal court ruled that the police officers who had questioned Stephen had committed substantial and significant breaches of the rules on interrogating suspects. The manner in which the confession was obtained made the conviction unsafe. He was released in January 2002, after serving 27 years in prison.

Don Hale's campaigning journalism and personal courage led to him receiving fifteen national and international awards, including Journalist of the Year and Man of the Year. He was awarded the OBE for his services to campaigning journalism. His book Town Without Pity became required reading for those officers who had to re-investigate Wendy Sewell's murder. This was in spite of the fact that some Derbyshire police officers still refer to Don as 'that mad bugger from Matlock'.

After a six-month reinvestigation of the case, Derbyshire Police announced in February 2003 that they had checked out other possible suspects in the case, and had found no evidence against them. The report concluded: 'The police are not looking for any other person for the murder of Wendy Sewell. All possible lines of enquiry have been exhausted. The case is now closed.' In their own words, 'Stephen Downing remains our only suspect.' However, to accept this version of events means believing that Stephen chose to spend 27 years in prison when he could have done ten years less simply by stating his guilt. It also means accepting that he committed a frenzied murder, and then calmly went home to see his mum and change his boots. We must also wonder why Don Hale was threatened and attacked during his seven-year campaign, if the real culprit wasn't frightened of what he might find out. It is possible that the crime was committed either by someone Wendy knew, perhaps after a lover's quarrel or in a fit of jealousy, or by someone acting on such a person's behalf.

Stephen Downing, after his release from 27 years in prison
(Derby Telegraph)

THE WINSTER DUEL

DR WILL CUDDIE MOVED TO WINSTER IN DERBYSHIRE WHEN HE WAS 27, HAVING PREVIOUSLY BEEN A SURGEON IN THE NAVY. HE GOT ON WELL WITH HIS PATIENTS, AND WAS POPULAR IN THE VILLAGE. HE WOULD GIVE MEDICAL ADVICE AND TREATMENT TO THE VILLAGERS, AND DID NOT CHARGE A FEE WHEN THE PATIENT WAS FROM A POOR FAMILY. ONE OF HIS PATIENTS WAS MARY BRITTLEBANK, THE DAUGHTER OF A WEALTHY LOCAL SOLICITOR. MARY AND WILLIAM BECAME FRIENDS, AND FOUND THEY WERE GROWING FONDER OF ONE ANOTHER. THEY BEGAN 'WALKING OUT'.

Back in the early years of the nineteenth century, a solicitor was a professional man, but medicine was not regarded as a professional occupation. To the Brittlebank family, the Scottish doctor was not of high enough status to be romantically involved with their daughter. Mary's brothers decided that they would have to act to put a stop to the unacceptable liaison between their sister and the doctor.

One Monday afternoon in May 1821 the doctor was walking through the village, accompanied by Mary, when they were accosted by her brother, William. William Brittlebank demanded that his sister come with him immediately, and ceased to associate with Will Cuddie. The doctor responded in language that owed much to his previous life in the navy. The two men exchanged angry words and parted on very bad terms.

That same evening, Will received a letter from his sweetheart's brother, demanding satisfaction for the insults he had received during their argument. He told the doctor to name a time and place when the matter could be settled by a duel. He said that if the doctor refused to meet him, he would publically denounce him as a coward.

Will Cuddie regarded the whole thing as preposterous, and ignored the letter, but he received a second written challenge the next morning. Again, the doctor ignored the foolish message. However, later that day, William Brittlebank turned up at Dr Cuddie's house, accompanied by his brothers Francis and Andrew and a friend, Edmund Spencer. Spencer went into the house and informed the young doctor that he must either apologise to William Brittlebank or fight a duel.

Will refused, but Spencer insisted. Reluctantly, the doctor agreed and went out into his garden, where the Brittlebank brothers were waiting. They had two loaded pistols with them. William took one and Will the other. William walked 15 yards, then turned and fired. Will Cuddie was shot in the abdomen, the bullet having lodged in his bowels. He died of his wound the next afternoon.

Bank House, the home of Dr Will Cuddie, in Winster.
The fatal duel took place in the back garden.

The village was outraged at the killing. The doctor had not wanted to fight a duel and had been coerced into it. They were even more outraged when a handwritten letter from Mary Brittlebank was found in Will's pocket after his death. In it she warned him to keep out of the way of her family 'as they are quite bent on shooting'. A rumour spread that only one of the duelling pistols had been loaded. It was whispered that the gun given to Dr Cuddie had been empty, though those present at the duel continued to claim that he had fired and missed.

An inquest found that the popular 31-year-old doctor had died through wilful murder. The brother who had fired the shot fled. Despite a £100 price on his head, he escaped to Australia, where he remained for the rest of his life. His other two brothers, Francis and Andrew, were tried for the murder along with Edmund Spencer, but were acquitted.

THE KILLING OF MEXICAN JOE

'MEXICAN JOE' TURNED UP IN THE SWADLINCOTE AREA IN NOVEMBER 1908, AND HE WAS AN IMMEDIATE SENSATION. THE FIRST THING TO POINT OUT ABOUT HIM WAS THAT HE WASN'T MEXICAN. INDEED, HE HAD A YORKSHIRE ACCENT. BUT HE WAS A MAN OF NO FIXED ABODE, A TRAVELLING ENTERTAINER. HE HAD SHOULDER-LENGTH HAIR AND HE WORE A CREAM-COLOURED HAT WITH A WIDE BRIM. BY SOUTH DERBYSHIRE STANDARDS HE WAS STRANGE AND EXOTIC AND THE LOCALS GAVE HIM AN EXOTIC NAME TO MATCH: HE BECAME MEXICAN JOE.

The first pub at which he turned up was the Cricketts Inn, Acresford. He approached the bar and seemed to conjure a glass tumbler from thin air. He put it on the bar and asked for a pint of ale. The barman was not used to customers who turned up with their own glass, but he filled it with beer. The stranger bent over and picked up the glass with his lips, not using his hands. He balanced the full tumbler of ale on his upturned face, then put it down again, still full of ale.

The other drinkers were amazed, and clapped and cheered at this display. He did an encore, this time with the whole of the top of the glass in his mouth. He appeared to drink, but again put the glass down still full. He then reached out his hand and produced an egg from nowhere. He put the egg in his mouth, then took a drink of his ale. His body began to shake, but as the onlookers watched, open-mouthed, thinking he was about to choke, he took the egg he'd just swallowed out of his ear. He produced a second egg from behind his head and a third from his blue-and-white handkerchief, and began to juggle with them. Somehow the flying eggs changed from three to six, seemingly in mid-air. The eggs transformed into billiard balls before their very eyes.

He finished his show, took off his hat and bowed. After his appreciative audience had cheered and whistled, a cap was passed round and a few small coins were thrown into it. He told them about his life on the road, performing his conjuring tricks at fairs and markets. He gathered up his belongings: some wooden sticks, a wooden box and a sack. Hoisting them over his shoulder, he left.

In the days that followed, he repeated his act at other pubs in the area: The Robin Hood in Overseal, the Mount Pleasant in Castle Gresley, the Coalminers Arms and the Granville Arms in Swadlincote. In a few hostelries he was shown the door, but in most he was a welcome visitor. A bit of entertainment went down well with the drinkers. He would use the little money he collected to buy food, and if he'd done particularly well, he would pay for a bed for the night. When he was short, however, he would hunker down and sleep in a jitty (an entry between houses) or in a warm brickyard. Usually he would walk everywhere, but if he was flush he would occasionally take a tram ride.

At the Victoria Inn in Church Gresley he added singing to his repertoire, giving a rendition of well-known music-hall songs. Returning to Swadlincote, he put on his conjuring display at the Stanhope Arms and the Barley Mow, before setting off for the Bull's Head. That was to be his last show.

In the early hours of the morning, the local bobby, PC Sheldon, was patrolling his patch when he was approached by a breathless John Palmer, the nightwatchman from Wragg's Brick and Pipeworks. Palmer told him that there was someone asleep in the building, and he thought it might be Jack James, a man the police were looking for, adding that he was probably drunk.

The policeman accompanied the nightwatchman to the building in question and approached the 'drunk'. It wasn't Jack James, however; it was Mexican Joe and he was dead. PC Sheldon removed the body by tying

The first local pub where Mexican Joe performedhis conjuring act was the Cricketts in Acresford

it with a clothesline to a trolley used in the factory for transporting bricks. It was taken to a makeshift mortuary situated under the town hall. All sorts of rumours spread through the town: Mexican Joe had committed suicide; he had been practising sword swallowing and the trick had gone wrong. However, all these topics of Swadlincote gossip were proved incorrect. The conjuror had been murdered.

The injuries on Mexican Joe's body included an almost severed thumb, along with wounds on his throat and head. The injury that had caused his death was a stab wound in the back of his neck which had severed his jugular vein. That could not have been self-inflicted and proved that he had been murdered. There had been no sign of the murder weapon at the scene of the killing.

The police questioned everyone who had seen Mexican Joe in the week before he was found dead, but got nowhere. Among Joe's few possessions, they found a poster advertising a show in Blackheath which included a stage magician called Herbert Nottingham. Could that have been Mexican Joe's real name? Because the dead man had spoken with a Yorkshire accent, the local police contacted their Yorkshire colleagues. These inquiries proved successful when a postman from Pontefract came down to Swadlincote and identified Mexican Joe as his 45-year-old brother. His real name was Herbert Nottingham Turner, and he had been a painter and joiner before the lure of a life on the road as a travelling conjuror had proved too strong. He had been leading a nomadic existence for many years, since leaving his native Yorkshire. At one time he had married and settled down, but his wife had died and he had gone back on the road.

Mexican Joe's funeral was held in Swadlincote on 28th November, and his coffin was carried on a horse-drawn hearse. The whole cost of the funeral was raised by South Derbyshire people. A number of locals attended his burial, but none of his own family. Perhaps they found their nomadic conjuror relation an embarrassment, someone not quite respectable.

The killer of Mexican Joe was never found. In addition, no clue to the killer's motive was ever discovered. The dead man had small copper coins to the value of four shillings on him when his body was found, so he had not been killed by a thief. Did some local person find his strange clothing and travelling lifestyle disturbing? Was it a case of simple prejudice against strangers? The motive, like the identity of the killer, has never been explained.

THE WINNATS PASS MURDERS

AT ONE TIME, PEAK FOREST IN DERBYSHIRE WAS THE PRIMARY DESTINATION FOR LOVERS WHO WANTED TO GET MARRIED WITHOUT THE CONSENT OF THEIR PARENTS. THE FACT THAT THE LOCAL CHAPEL LAY INSIDE THE BOUNDARIES OF THE ROYAL FOREST MEANT THAT THE LOCAL PRIEST COULD MARRY COUPLES IMMEDIATELY WITHOUT THE NEED FOR BANNS. IT WAS A FAST, NO-QUESTIONS-ASKED CEREMONY, BUT OWING TO AN ANOMALY IN THE LAW IT WAS LEGAL AND BINDING. IT WAS DERBYSHIRE'S OWN GRETNA GREEN. NOT SURPRISINGLY, MANY COUPLES MADE THEIR WAY TO PEAK FOREST. THE MARRIAGE ACT OF 1753 SHOULD HAVE PUT AN END TO THE PRACTICE, BUT IT CONTINUED ON A LESSER SCALE. THE LAST COUPLE MARRIED THERE IN THIS WAY WAS AS LATE AS 1938.

One such couple who decided to travel there were Alan and Clara. Clara was from a wealthy family. Although Alan was from a good family, they were much poorer. Clara's parents had disapproved of the match and forbidden Clara to see her young man. The two decided to elope, and to head for Peak Forest where they could be married without the consent of her father.

It was April 1758 when they set out on horseback. When they reached Castleton, they called in at an inn to rest and to ask for directions. There they were observed by a boisterous quartet of local lead miners – John Bradshaw, Nick Cook, Tom Hall and Frank Butler – who were drinking in the bar. The men quietened down and eavesdropped as the landlord gave the couple directions, advising them to head down Winnats Pass, a rocky ravine just a mile or so along the road. The men noticed the good clothes that the strangers were wearing, and speculated that they might be carrying a large amount of money. When the couple went into another room to eat a meal, the four young miners resumed their drinking, getting so rowdy that the landlord eventually threw them out.

This was an era when strangers were looked on with suspicion and mistrust, and as a possible source of ill-gotten gains for those who were not averse to violent crime. These 'strangers' need not be from distant parts; they could just as easily be from a town a few miles away or a village just up the road. They were not from Castleton, so they were foreign. It was a very parochial time.

The four men decided to wait for the young lovers to set out again on their journey and to waylay them. They picked up a fifth man, Jim Ashton, and armed themselves with pickaxe handles. They headed for

Winnats Pass and there they waited. After an hour or so, they saw Alan and Clara riding into the rocky ravine. Yelling and cursing, they leapt out and pulled the man and girl from their horses, which quickly bolted back towards Castleton. The men roughly searched Alan and Clara, and shouted with delight when they discovered that they were carrying no less than £200.

The terrified couple were pushed into a barn, while the lead miners discussed what they could do with this newly acquired fortune of £40 each. When the men re-entered the barn, Alan begged them to spare his and Clara's lives, but the men just stared at him without speaking. Realising that the men would not show any mercy, Alan hurled himself at them. His reward was to be clubbed to death. Clara watched in horror as her lover died, and then suffered the same fate. The men left the two dead bodies in the barn overnight, but the next day they disposed of them by throwing them down a disused mine shaft nearby. When the riderless horses arrived back in Castleton, it was realised that the young couple had perished, but the exact method of their death was not known.

The murderers did not enjoy their new wealth. A year after the brutal murders, John Bradshaw met an early death, being killed by falling rocks, and Nicholas Cook died when he fell from a buttress. Both of these accidents occurred in Winnats Pass, which raises issues of ironic justice and the possibility of the very rocks themselves wreaking revenge on the guilty men. Tom Hall and Frank Butler found the knowledge of what they had

Winnats Pass
Shutterstock/Kevin Eaves (top) and Shutterstock/ Equlibrium Photographers (bottom)

done too much to bear, the former committing suicide and the latter going insane. The fifth man – Jim Ashton – used his share of the loot to go into the horse-trading business, but without success. All his horses fell ill and died. It was Ashton who left a deathbed confession to the robbery and murders, naming the others as his partners in crime.

The skeletons of the murdered lovers were discovered ten years after the crime, and they were interred in St Edmund's churchyard in Castleton. The red Morocco leather saddle from Clara's horse can be seen on display in the little museum in the entrance of Speedwell Cavern.

AN EIGHTEEN-YEAR STRUGGLE FOR JUSTICE

LYNN SIDDONS WAS GRANNY-REARED. TO HER, FLO AND FRED SIDDONS WERE MAM AND DAD, ALTHOUGH SHE KNEW THAT HER BIG SISTER GAIL WAS HER BIOLOGICAL MOTHER. THE FAMILY LIVED IN CARLYLE STREET ON THE SINFIN ESTATE ON THE SOUTH SIDE OF DERBY.

At school, Lynn was bright but not really interested in academic study. She was good at English and Art, and always enjoyed PE and Games. She left school at Easter 1978, at the age of sixteen, and had a job in the local co-op butchers to take up after she had enjoyed the Easter holiday. On Easter Monday, she was expecting her boyfriend Bobby to come round, and that they would be going to the fair. When Bobby didn't turn up, she walked down the street to visit a friend, Roy Brookes. Roy, who was fifteen but looked about twelve, lived with his mother Dot and stepfather Mick at number 27.

Roy told Lynn that he was going out to walk to a farm where he might get a part-time job, and asked Lynn to come with him. She liked Roy – she had often stuck up for him when he was teased for being mixed-race – and willingly agreed. The two of them set off through Red Wood. What Roy knew, but not Lynn, was that his stepfather was following them. Mick Brookes was an odd man, and Lynn found him creepy. He had an unpleasant attitude to women. One small example was his habit of putting photos of girls on his dartboard and throwing darts and knives at them.

When Flo Siddons got home that afternoon, she found that Lynn had gone out. As Lynn's purse was still on the table and she hadn't left a note, Flo guessed that she wasn't far away and would soon be back. She went round to see Roy Brookes, who told her that he and Lynn had been walking through Red Wood, but he'd needed to nip behind some trees to answer a call of nature, and when he came back Lynn had gone off without him.

During the evening, Flo began to worry. Members of the Siddons family gathered and began to go out into the estate and the wood to search for the missing girl. At 10pm, she rang the police, who dismissed her anxiety. The girl was sixteen, they said. It was a bank holiday. She had obviously met a lad or a group of friends and she was out enjoying herself. She would be home when she was ready. Flo knew that they were not describing Lynn, who always let her know where she was.

As days passed with no sign of Lynn, Flo decided – not for the last time – that if you needed something doing, you had better do it yourself. She had photos of the missing girl printed onto leaflets and the family gave them out at the fair. Flo's other daughter, Cynthia, got in touch with her MP, Phillip Whitehead, a former television producer and journalist. He had contacts in the press, and the Saturday edition of the Derby Telegraph had a front-page item about the missing girl.

The body of Lynn Siddons was discovered the next day by an off-duty police cadet. She was lying near to the towpath of the Trent and Mersey canal. At first, it was thought she had been shot with a shotgun, judging by the number of wounds on her body, but a post-mortem found that they were multiple stab wounds. Some were superficial pinpricks, but four were deep four-inch penetrating wounds that had caused her death. There was also evidence that she had been half-strangled by someone standing behind her.

The police took Roy Brookes into custody, but they could get nothing out of him. He sobbed and refused to speak to them. As they were getting nowhere, the police took what turned out to be a foolish decision. They allowed Mick Brookes to have ten minutes alone with his stepson. After speaking to Mick, Roy now stated that he had killed Lynn because she was teasing him. He had acted alone, and nobody had witnessed the attack.

The police decided that they had got the killer and Roy Brookes was charged. No one seemed to have any concerns over to how a small boy weighing less than six-and-a-half stone could subdue and murder a fit, strong girl who was four inches taller than himself.

At his trial in November, Roy Brookes was the accused and Mick Brookes gave evidence for the prosecution. Roy now told a different story, saying that his stepfather had caught up with him and Lynn by the canal, and had produced a carving knife. He had seized Lynn from behind and ordered Roy to stab the girl. Terrified, he did so, but only pricking her skin. He then took the decision to break the knife to stop Mick from harming her further. However, Mick produced a second knife and stabbed the girl to death. It was obvious to the jury that this scenario fitted the forensic evidence and after deliberating for only twenty minutes, they found the boy not guilty. The judge ordered Roy to be taken to a place of safety for his own protection.

To the astonishment of the whole of Derby, including Lynn's family, Mick Brookes was not arrested and charged. He just went home – and his home was only a few doors away from the Siddons house. This situation

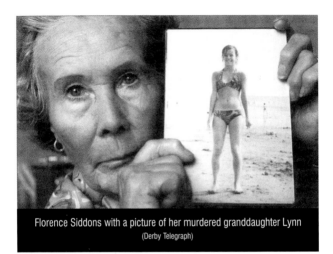

Florence Siddons with a picture of her murdered granddaughter Lynn
(Derby Telegraph)

went on for some years. The police continued to say that there was insufficient evidence to charge Michael Brookes. Flo knew who had killed her granddaughter, but he remained a free man.

Remembering her earlier lesson, Flo's family decided to take action themselves. Petitions were circulated, marches were organised, and Mick Brookes was hounded first from Sinfin, then from his new home in the city centre. The Siddons family and their neighbours had no compunction about their vendetta. They knew Brookes was guilty of murder and he was getting away with it. Two years later, Flo's daughter Cynthia was charged with trying to run down Michael Brookes with her car. The charge of attempted murder was reduced to one of reckless driving, and she was fined.

A breakthrough seemed to have been made in 1980 when Mick Brookes made the fatal mistake of leaving his wife Dot for a younger woman. Hell has no fury like a woman scorned. Dot contacted the Siddons, and three women – Flo, Gail and Cynthia – went to visit her. Dot told them that Brookes had confessed to murdering Lynn, and that she was willing to make a statement. It was arranged for a retired police officer to visit Dot Brookes and the statement was taken down and signed. In it Dot told how Michael Brookes had confessed to the murder, before burning the clothes he had been wearing that day. He said that Roy had been present but had been trembling and useless. When Dot had asked him why he had done it, Michael Brookes had said that Lynn was 'a slut, like the rest of them'.

Dot repeated this statement to Phillip Whitehead's researcher, and it was immediately handed over to the police. It seemed to Flo Siddons that the police were bound to act, but things went wrong. Once he heard about his wife's statement, Michael abandoned his new girlfriend and returned to Dot. In return, Dot withdrew her statement.

In 1981, the campaigning journalist Paul Foot became involved, using his column in the Daily Mirror to review the case. By referring to the court case where Cynthia had been charged with reckless driving, Foot was able to give the background to the case and – most importantly

– to name Michael Brookes. Paul Foot stated that his intervention was justified because of 'the incompetence of the police, the battle for justice by this determined family, but most of all, you had a murder where everyone knew the suspects but they were still free'. He also gave Flo Siddons the name of a young solicitor, Jane Deighton, who might help her. Jane came up with what at first seemed an outrageous suggestion. Flo and her family should sue Michael and Roy Brookes in a civil court for damages caused by Lynn's death. The people of Derby helped to raise funds for the case, holding jumble sales, a sponsored walk and pub quizzes.

In court, Roy recalled the events again, saying that his stepfather had an obsession with knifes and had boasted that he wanted to kill more women than Jack the Ripper. Roy said he had seen him stab Lynn to death and hide her body in undergrowth near the canal towpath. Michael Brookes opted not to give evidence. The judge gave his verdict: the case was proved and Flo's family was awarded £10,641 in damages. This nominal sum broke Flo's heart, but the amount was unimportant. In his summary, the judge had stated that Michael Brookes had killed Lynn, and that Roy had taken part under duress.

This civil case did force the hand of the police, but it was 1992 – fourteen years after the murder – before the police eventually arrested Michael Brookes, charging him with murder, and it was a further four years before the case came to court. This time Mick Brookes was the accused and it was Roy who was a witness for the prosecution. After a thirty-four-day trial the jury took nine hours to reach their verdict, but this time it was one of guilty. Eighteen years after he had murdered Lynn Siddons, Michael Brookes was sentenced to life imprisonment. Flo Siddons' long and courageous struggle to bring her granddaughter's killer to justice had finally come to a successful conclusion.

CIRCUMSTANTIAL EVIDENCE

IN AUGUST 1846, TWO MEN WERE USING BUCKETS TO EMPTY A CESSPIT BELONGING TO A CHESTERFIELD FLOUR MERCHANT, GEORGE BUNTING, WHEN THEY NOTICED SOME BONES AMONG THE MANURE. AT FIRST THEY TOOK THEM TO BE ANIMAL BONES, BUT WHEN THEY DISCOVERED SOME REMNANTS OF CLOTHING, THEY TOOK A CLOSER LOOK. SOME OF THE BONES LOOKED LIKE PARTS OF A HUMAN BEING. A THIRD MAN WHO HAD BEEN SPREADING THE MANURE FROM THE CESSPIT ONTO GEORGE BUNTING'S FIELD HAD ALSO FOUND SOME RIB BONES AND MORE PIECES OF CLOTHING. THEY INFORMED MR BUNTING, WHO FETCHED IN TWO FRIENDS WHO HAPPENED TO BE A BUTCHER AND A DOCTOR. THEY CONFIRMED THAT THESE WERE INDEED HUMAN REMAINS. WHEN THE BONES WERE ASSEMBLED, IT WAS FOUND THAT THEY CONSTITUTED A VIRTUALLY COMPLETE HUMAN SKELETON. THE SKULL APPEARED TO BE FRACTURED IN THREE PLACES, WHICH WAS THOUGHT TO INDICATE THE POSSIBILITY OF FOUL PLAY, RATHER THAN AN ACCIDENT OR SUICIDE.

The cesspit had last been emptied in June the previous year, so the body must have been put in the pit since then. The authorities wondered whether there might be a connection to the disappearance of a local man, George Collis, who had not been seen since December 1845. Both his mother, Mary, and his girlfriend, Ellen, had been totally mystified and bewildered by his sudden absence. They were shown the clothing found in the pit, and confirmed that these were the clothes the 26-year-old was wearing on the last day they had seen him.

Police established that George had been seen leaving his girlfriend's house at 6.30pm on Sunday 7th December, and had been seen later in a shop belonging to Joe Morley in the Shambles district of the town. The Shambles was an area where animals were slaughtered and meat was sold. George was arguing with his business partner, John Platts. The two men were partners in a butchery business, John providing the butchery skills and George the finance. The passer-by said that Platts was holding a butcher's axe at the time. As he walked on, the witness said, he had heard the sound of something in the shop falling, and then the door was slammed shut.

Half an hour later, a man saw two men half carrying what looked like a drunken man from Morley's shop to Platts' own shop. Other witnesses reported that on the evening of the following day, they had seen three men carrying a heavy sack, which they assumed to be full of offal. The men took their sack into Bunting's yard, where the cesspit was situated. One of the men was John Platts, the second was Joe Morley, and the third was a stranger. After his partner's disappearance John Platts began telling people that George Collis had left Chesterfield and gone to Manchester.

After the identification of George Collis as the body in Bunting's cesspit, the police began to focus on John Platts as the man to question. He denied killing his business partner. John Platts said that on the night that George Collis disappeared, he had an alibi as he had been in the Old Angel pub from 6pm until closing time. He also stated that George had borrowed £2.10s 0d on the night he disappeared, adding that George now owed him a total of £9. George's family found that difficult to believe as they knew the debt – far more than £9 – was the other way round. The police searched Platts' house and found a pocket watch and a pair of boots that were known to belong to the dead man. Platts claimed that he had bought the watch from a local villain known as Lanky Bill, a fact that Lanky Bill vehemently denied when the police questioned him. The publican of the Old Angel also contradicted John Platts' story that he had spent five hours there on the night George had vanished. The truth was that Platts had only been in the pub from 9.30pm.

John Platts was arrested and charged with the murder of George Collis. His trial was held in Derby the following

March. The prosecution alleged that Platts had killed his partner, either in Joe Morley's butchers shop or in his own, and had then dismembered his body. He and two henchmen had put the body parts into a sack and dumped it in the cesspit belonging to the flour merchant. One of the men seen carrying the sack, Joe Morley, had since died, and couldn't be questioned, and the third man was never traced. The motive was possibly that the two men had argued over money owed by Platts to Collis, and killing his business partner was one way for John Platts to cancel the debt.

Although all the evidence was circumstantial, the jury took only minutes to find the accused man guilty of murder, and the judge, Mr Justice Patterson, sentenced him to death. In the days before the hanging, John Platts wrote a confession that he was present when George Collis was killed, but said the actual murder and dismemberment of the body was done by Morley and the third unidentified man.

Platts was executed at a public hanging held outside Derby Prison on 1st April 1847 before a crowd of many thousands. Many of them were from Chesterfield, and had travelled down to Derby especially to see John Platts pay the price of his crime.

DEATH OF A REPTON BAKER

ON A GRAVESTONE IN REPTON CHURCHYARD, THE FOLLOWING WORDS ARE INSCRIBED:

To the memory of Samuel Marshall who unfortunately fell victim to a barbarous assassin on February 14th 1786, in the 21st year of his age.

By murderous hand my thread of life was broke Dreadful the hour and terrible the stroke Repent thou wicked spoiler of my youth Behold me here, consider my parents both See from thy bloody hand what woes arise While calls for vengeance pierce the lofty skies Thou too must suffer, though thou escape the laws For God is just and will avenge my cause.

This epitaph, composed by a master at Repton School, refers to a murder of a local baker on Valentine's Day in 1786.

Young Samuel Marshall worked in the family bakery business in Repton. On Saturday 14th February 1786, after crossing the River Trent by the ferry, he had made deliveries of bread and cakes to Willington, then headed west to Rolleston and other villages. He was returning to Repton, carrying the money he had collected, which was later estimated to be in the region of £7, a considerable sum in the eighteenth century. He got only as far as the bridge over the canal in Willington before meeting his tragic end at the hands of a robber. His body was discovered by a labourer from Ticknall at 7pm. Samuel had suffered a severe blow to the head and his throat had been cut. His pockets had been turned out and emptied.

A hue and cry was raised by the Justices of the Peace, and a handbill was issued offering a reward of £40. A blacksmith's hammer was discovered, which had been thrown over a hedge near the murder site, and it was immediately thought to be one of the weapons used on Samuel Marshall.

The authorities went to question the Rolleston blacksmith, who stated that he had lent the hammer to a young man named James Wheldon a few days earlier. Wheldon denied that he had ever borrowed a hammer from the blacksmith, but was not believed. On Thursday 19th February, Wheldon was arrested and charged with the murder. A local magistrate, Sir Robert Burdett, questioned him for eight hours, then committed him for trial.

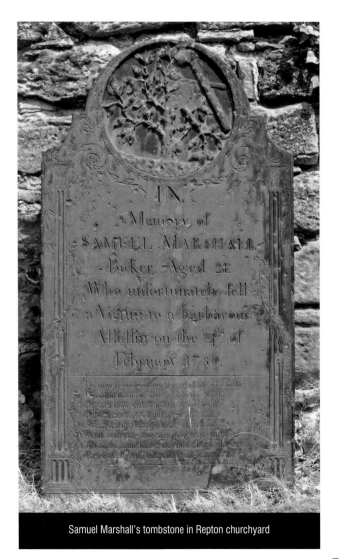

Samuel Marshall's tombstone in Repton churchyard

In March, James Wheldon appeared at the Derby Assizes, but after a six-hour hearing he was found not guilty of the murder. He had been given an alibi by a young lady from Barrow-upon-Trent. Given that the girl was his fiancée, this might not have been enough on its own to earn him an acquittal, but the Rolleston blacksmith who had earlier stated that he had lent the hammer to the accused man now refused to swear to this in court. The alibi, plus the fact that there was no longer any sworn evidence connecting James Wheldon to the hammer used in the killing, was enough to persuade the court to set him free.

However, it was noted that in the years that followed James Wheldon used to visit the gravestone of the murdered Samuel Marshall to gaze at it. Could it have been simply respect, or was there an element of guilt? The fact remains that the murder of the young baker from Repton is one that must go down as unsolved.

Above the inscription on the gravestone is the image of a tree with six branches, one of them broken. This almost certainly refers to the fact that Samuel was one of six boys, all of whom worked in the family business.

FAMILY MASSACRE IN EASTMOOR

IN EARLY JANUARY 1977, TWO WARDERS WERE TAKING A MALE PRISONER NAMED BILLY HUGHES BY TAXI FROM LEICESTER GAOL TO CHESTERFIELD, WHERE HE WAS APPEAR IN COURT, CHARGED WITH GBH AND ASSAULT. BEFORE THE TAXI REACHED CHESTERFIELD, THE 30-YEAR-OLD PRISONER PRODUCED A KITCHEN KNIFE. HE STABBED ONE WARDER THEN FORCED THE TAXI DRIVER TO DRIVE HIM THROUGH CHESTERFIELD AND OUT TOWARDS ASHOVER. THERE HE FORCED THE DRIVER AND WARDERS TO GET OUT, AND DROVE OFF IN THE TAXI. AFTER HE SKIDDED ON ICE AND CRASHED THE TAXI INTO A WALL NEAR BEELEY, HE ABANDONED IT AND SET OUT ON FOOT OVER THE MOORS, A DESPERATE HIKE IN THE JANUARY ICE AND SNOW.

Three hours later he reached the A619, the road from Chesterfield to Baslow. He came up to a row of three cottages at Eastmoor. The middle cottage was empty, but after arming himself with two axes from an outhouse, he knocked on the door of one of the occupied cottages. Pottery Cottage was the home of five people: Arthur and Amy Minton, their daughter Gill and son-in-law Richard, and their ten-year-old granddaughter Sarah.

When Billy Hughes pushed his way into their cottage, with an axe in either hand, the only two at home were Arthur and Amy, aged 72 and 68 respectively. He quickly took them prisoner, and added a boning knife from the kitchen to his stock of weapons. Gill Moran got home from work at 3pm, to find that she was the third member of her family to be taken hostage by a desperate – and armed – escaped prisoner. He added young Sarah to his captives when she came home from school. To spare her feelings, Gill told her daughter that Hughes was a driver whose car had broken down and who was waiting for help.

Sarah went up to her room, but when Richard Moran got home from work, Hughes assembled the whole family together downstairs. Using a washing line and electric flex, he tied up each member of the family, binding their hands and feet, and also gagging them. He carried Richard Moran upstairs and left him on a bed, then did the same to Gill, Amy and Sarah. He left each of them in a different room.

Pottery Cottage, Eastmoor

He returned to Arthur, the only member of the family left downstairs. With the boning knife, he killed the man, and then hid his body under a coat. The brutal and callous killer then went upstairs and killed Sarah. Because each family member was stored in a separate room, he was able to keep up the pretence that they were all still alive, and would remain so if each of them obeyed his instructions.

The next day, Gill did as instructed, ringing her office and Sarah's school to say that they were both ill and would not be coming in. Hughes even sent Gill into Chesterfield to buy him cigarettes, newspapers and a camping stove, telling her that she should bear in mind that her family's lives were in his hands. The cruel and heartless monster even told Gill she should buy a present for her daughter, who was in reality lying dead in an upstairs room.

While she was away, Hughes hid Gill's father's body in an annex. On her return he instructed her to cook soup for everyone. He even took some to Sarah and Arthur's rooms, still pretending that they were alive. Gill and Richard, and Gill's mother Amy, co-operated fully with all he said, believing that they were protecting Arthur and young Sarah.

The police were, of course, searching for their escaped prisoner, and had set up an incident room in The Highwayman pub just a hundred yards from where the family were being held in Pottery Cottage.

Full of bravado, Hughes forced Richard and Gill to drive him to Richard's factory in Staveley to collect £200 of wages from his office. Back at Pottery Cottage, Billy Hughes tied up Richard and Amy. He packed a suitcase and threw it into the Morans' car. Taking Gill with him, he drove off, but after two miles he turned back and returned to the cottage. Leaving Gill in the car, he went in, saying that he was going to find an atlas, but what he did was far more harrowing. He went to the room where Amy Minton was tied up and cut her throat. He then did the same to her son-in-law, Richard. He then heard the sound of a car being driven away at speed. It was the couple from the other cottage, both teachers. Guessing that they had found out about the situation and were going for help, he drove off, with Gill Moran still a hostage.

The neighbours had by now rung the police and a twenty-mile car chase ensued. Eventually, up on Tideswell Moor, Hughes was stopped, but holding an axe to Gill Moran's throat he commandeered the police car and drove off in that. Followed by a large number of police cars, he drove over the Cat and Fiddle pass before crashing the car.

A 45-minute standoff took place, while officers tried to get the man to release his hostage. At the same time armed officers were quietly getting into place, using the stone walls as cover. When Hughes eventually lost patience and raised his axe to kill Gill Moran, the marksmen opened fire, killing their target. An inquest brought in a verdict that he had died through justifiable homicide.

Billy Hughes was due to be buried in his home village of Boythorpe, but on the day of his funeral the villagers

– including teenagers from William Rhodes School – took direct action and filled in the grave before the hearse got there. Realising that the people of Boythorpe did not want this obnoxious killer buried among them, the authorities had a change of mind and arranged for him to be cremated instead. The headmaster of William Rhodes School reprimanded the students who had used their lunchtime to fill in the intended grave, but I am sure that their parents thought their children had done the right thing.

'AN UNDULY LENIENT VERDICT'

AMONG THE MEN DRINKING IN THE STANHOPE ARMS IN NEWHALL ON 4TH FEBRUARY 1841 WERE FOUR COLLIERS WHO HAD AN INTEREST – A PASTIME – IN COMMON. THE MEN WERE JOHN ADEY, HENRY HOSKISON, ROBERT STALEY AND HARRY EAMES. THEY WERE DRINKING AND OPENLY DISCUSSING THEIR PLANS FOR THE REST OF THE EVENING. THEY WOULD GO INTO NEWHALL MANOR, PART OF THE BRETBY PARK ESTATE, AND GET THEMSELVES A HARE OR TWO. THEIR COMMON INTEREST WAS POACHING.

During the evening, two of them – John and Henry – each left the pub in turn and each came back with a gun, which they proceeded to load. It was observed that Henry Hoskison was putting a double load of powder into his gun, and one of his companions laughed and said the he was putting a 'rum-un' in. Henry agreed, adding that if he fired it it 'would make his jaw ring'. The four men continued drinking until 10.30pm, then left to enjoy a night's fun and delight in the snow-covered local terrain.

When they got to Mr Abbott's turnip field, they spotted a hare. Adey and Staley waited on the road while Hoskison and Eames went into the field in pursuit of their prey. When Adey thought he'd seen a dog he turned back, leaving the armed Henry Hoskison on his own.

The greatest enemies of the poaching fraternity were the gamekeepers, employed by the landowners to protect their game, because if a rabbit or hare was on his land, the animal itself became private property. The estate owners did not want some local miners or other working men trespassing on their land to get some meat for the pot.

Patrolling the manor that night were two keepers, George Hill and his assistant Robert Harvey. After meeting up with Harvey for a smoke and a conversation near to a pottery, George Hill set off on his own. He soon spotted the four Newhall colliers, and noticed that two of them were armed. As he watched, two of the poachers went into a turnip field, the other pair continuing to walk along the path. George Hill hurried back to find his colleague, and to pick up his club.

The Stanhope Arms in Newhall was in a row of three: the Angel, the Stanhope and the Hollybush
(Graham Nutt/Magic Attic Local History Archive, Swadlincote)

Robert Harvey followed the two men across the field, while George Hill tracked the other pair.

Suddenly George heard a shot and hastened across the turnip field. There he found the body of his fellow keeper, lying on his back, and with his clothing smouldering and burning. He did what he could for the man but it was to no avail. Robert had been shot dead at close range, and the flash of the powder had set light to his clothes. George attempted to put out the flames by covering them with snow, before going to find the local constable.

A surgeon – Mr John Johnson of St Alkmund's in Derby – examined the body the next day, and reported: 'The body was very much burnt. I found a wound on the left side of the chest, a little below the collar bone. I opened the chest and found the wound passing along the upper portion of the left lobe of the lungs, wounding the large vessels of the heart, dislocating and fracturing the back bone, in which I found lodged a considerable quantity of shot. The shot was not at all scattered; it was lodged in the space of an inch. The wound must have caused instant death. I should say from the nature of the wound that the gun must have been fired close to the deceased. I should think the shot was more than a common charge.'

On the morning of 6th February, the constable went to the home of John Adey, who seems to have been very willing to give the names of his fellow poachers, though he later denied in court that this had anything to do with the reward offered for the name of the killer. The constable immediately went to a cabin at the local colliery, where he apprehended the other three men. He then proceeded to the home of Henry Hoskison, where he seized a gun, a bag of shot and a flask of powder.

The trial of Henry Hoskison, charged with murder, was held in March. Much of the evidence was not contested. All the jury had to decide was whether Hoskison had deliberately fired at the keeper, or whether the two men were struggling for possession of it when it went off. Several witnesses gave evidence as to the character of the 23-year-old accused man. Several witnesses –

innkeeper Tom Thornewell, bricklayer Robert Peace, farmer William Abbot and others – all gave evidence of the previous good character and kind nature of Henry Hoskison. Benjamin Bridge, a smith, said that he had known Henry from childhood and knew him to be of a good, kind disposition and humane conduct.

The jury considered all the evidence and came to the conclusion that the gun had gone off during a struggle. They found Henry guilty of manslaughter but not guilty of murder. This outraged the judge, who had been ready with a death sentence. He commented bitterly that the jury had given the prisoner the benefit of the doubt whereas he himself could not help thinking the he had deliberately shot the deceased. He added that he had never met with any case that called for a more severe sentence than what he could now give for manslaughter.

Still grumbling that the verdict was unduly lenient, he said that he would pass the maximum verdict allowed for manslaughter. He sentenced Henry Hoskison to be transported 'beyond the seas for the term of his life'. A month later the young collier was transported to Australia on a ship called the Westmoreland. He was put to work in a coalmine in Tasmania and died there in 1851.

THE SIMMONDLEY PIT MURDERS

ALBERT BURROWS HAD A SOCIAL AND FINANCIAL PROBLEM, BASED ON THE FACT THAT HE HAD TWO WIVES AND FAMILIES, EACH UNKNOWN TO THE OTHER. HE HAD A WIFE AND DAUGHTER AT HOME IN GLOSSOP, BUT IN 1918, WHILE WORKING AWAY IN CHESHIRE, HE HAD MARRIED A 27-YEAR-OLD WOMAN CALLED HANNAH CALLADINE. HANNAH HAD A YOUNG DAUGHTER, ELSIE, FROM A PREVIOUS RELATIONSHIP, BUT IT WAS NOT LONG BEFORE SHE HAD A YOUNG SON TOO, NAMED ALBERT AFTER HIS FATHER.

Albert Burroughs and Hannah Calladine
(Glossop Heritage Centre)

For a while, Burrows ran two families, one in Cheshire and one in Glossop, and sent money to both wives. However, after the war ended, work became hard to find and the payments stopped. He had told Hannah that he was a widower with a daughter living in Glossop, but his second 'wife' became suspicious and wrote to the daughter. The daughter passed the letter to her mother, and Albert's secret was exposed. In February 1919 Albert Burrows was charged with committing bigamy, and was given a sentence of six months in prison. When he had served his sentence, he returned to Glossop to live with his legitimate wife and daughter, abandoning Hannah to try to bring up Albert and Elsie on her own. He was supposed to pay her seven shillings a week, but he never made any attempt to do so. As a result, he was again arrested and sentenced to prison, this time for 21 days.

His next attempt to solve his problem led him to go and fetch his second family from Cheshire and bring them to Glossop, suggesting to his wife that both families should live together in one happy household! Hannah could get a job to earn money while the original Mrs Burrows looked after all the children. For some reason Mrs Burrows objected to this arrangement and took herself off to stay with a friend. Burrows then settled down with Hannah, baby Albert and stepdaughter Elsie in his Glossop house. He could not find a job, but Hannah began to work in a local paper mill. Were his problems solved? No. This time it was his first wife who took out a summons for maintenance.

On 12th January 1919, he appeared in court and told the magistrates that matters had settled themselves, because Hannah had moved to Manchester and taken the two children with her. To many, this seemed suspiciously convenient for Albert Burrows. He had been seen early one morning leading his stepdaughter by the hand, and telling neighbours that he was taking her to be with her mother. These seemingly innocent words were later proved to have a chilling and callous meaning. He had killed Hannah and baby Albert, hidden their bodies, and he was indeed taking little Elsie 'to be with her mother'.

Four days later, his wife moved back in with him. She may have thought it odd that Hannah had left her belongings behind, including her wedding ring. Burrows immediately began to destroy all letters and papers relating to Hannah and her family. Eventually the local gossip about Hannah died down and the Burrows family began to lead a relatively normal life. Albert even found some casual work on a farm. He had 'got away with it', it seemed.

However, on Sunday 4th March 1923, an alarming event took place when a four-year-old boy named Tommy Woods disappeared. The whole of Glossop began to take part in a search. One of the most avid searchers was

Albert Burrows, but the policeman in charge, Inspector Chadwick, was somewhat cynical about Albert's sudden display of community spirit. A farm labourer named Sam Robinson told Inspector Chadwick that at 11.30am on the Sunday, he had seen Burrows at Bridgefield, holding the hand of a little boy. As the man and boy had not been seen on any of the roads in the area, the inspector concluded that Burrows and the boy must have headed across the high moors overlooking Hargate Hill and Simmondley village.

Next, Inspector Chadwick went to interview another farmworker, Frank Burgess, who had seen Burrows an hour later, alone on Hargate Hill. Frank took the policeman to the spot where he'd seen Burrows, and on the way, the inspector spotted an old airshaft belonging to a disused mine. He took a closer look and noticed that the 6' 6" wall around it had some loose stones. He removed a few, leaned through, and he could hear the faint sound of running water some hundred feet below. Frank told him that his employer regularly used this shaft to dispose of rubbish.

Chadwick re-interviewed Albert Burrows, who now said that on the Sunday in question he had seen Tommy Woods in Hollincross Lane. He had taken him across the fields looking for thrushes' nests. When they got up on the moors, he'd left Tommy sitting on his own while he went to try to find a rabbit. He was only about forty yards away, but when he returned the boy had gone. He shouted for a few minutes before walking home.

A search was made in the area and a second old mineshaft was discovered. This one was not properly fenced off, except for a few wooden posts with rusty barbed wire strands between them. The police used grappling irons and a rope in a vain attempt to investigate the shaft, but the rope broke and it was decided to resume the investigation the next day. However, overnight Inspector Chadwick remembered the first airshaft he'd seen, the one with a high wall around it. He decided that the police search would begin with that shaft, the one near Cloud Farm.

The following morning, a platform was erected over the airshaft, and grappling hooks were lowered into the depths. On the second attempt, Tommy Woods' body was discovered. As the news spread that the boy's body had been found, the villagers had no doubts as to who was responsible. A mob of angry men armed themselves with sticks and managed to track down Albert Burrows. They had tied his hands, and were about to string him up from a tree when the police arrived and took him into custody.

Once at the police station, Albert Edward Burrows was charged with murder and sent for trial at Derby Assizes. Out of the blue, Inspector Chadwick asked, 'Burrows, what became of Hannah Calladine?' Burrows blustered that Hannah had obtained a good job in Manchester, earning decent money. The inspector remained unconvinced. Could the bodies of Hannah and her two children be at the bottom of the same airshaft where little Tommy Woods had met his untimely death?

The police returned to the shaft where the boy's body had been found, and a more thorough investigation began. The shaft had flooded and a steam pump was used to lower the water level. Men then went down the shaft with shovels. Eventually they came across a portion of a child's skull and part of a woman's torso. More human remains were discovered, including the tibia and

Police begin the search of the airshaft at Simmondley pit
(Glossop Heritage Centre)

fibula bones of a young girl, and an adult female skull. Examination of the teeth and the clothing attached to the bones proved that these were the remains of Hannah Calladine and her two children.

At the trial of Albert Burrows, the prosecution decided for some reason to proceed with only two charges: the murders of Hannah and little Albert. The jury deliberated for only 12 minutes before bringing in a unanimous verdict of guilty. Albert Edward Burrows was sentenced to death, and was hanged at Bagthorpe prison at 8am on Wednesday 8th August 1923.

It is rather worrying to think that if Burrows had not killed the boy, and thrown his body into the same airshaft where he had disposed of the bodies of his three previous victims, then it is likely that he would have got away with his crimes.

'BESSIE GOODWIN WAS MY PROPERTY'

WHEN ELIZABETH GOODWIN WAS TWENTY YEARS OLD, SHE MOVED TO LIVE WITH HER GRANDFATHER, CAPTAIN FRANCIS GREEN GOODWIN OF WIGWELL HALL, NEAR WIRKSWORTH. CAPTAIN GOODWIN WAS A WELL-RESPECTED MAN IN THE AREA, AND AN ACTIVE MAGISTRATE, THOUGH WELL INTO HIS EIGHTIES BY THEN. SHORTLY BEFORE SHE MOVED TO LIVE WITH HER GRANDFATHER, ELIZABETH HAD BECOME ENGAGED TO GEORGE TOWNLEY, A WELL-EDUCATED MAN FROM HENDHAM VALE, NEAR MANCHESTER. ELIZABETH HAD MET GEORGE THROUGH HER UNCLE, WHO WAS A DOCTOR TO THE TOWNLEY FAMILY.

Wigwell Hall, now called Wigwell Grange
(Peter Barrs/Geograph)

However, Captain Goodwin did not think George Townley was a good match for his granddaughter, and when a local clergyman began to visit Elizabeth, the captain gave his blessing to the new suitor instead. Elizabeth too decided that she preferred the young clergyman who was now paying her attention. She therefore wrote to George Townley and asked him to set her free from her engagement, and to return her letters to him.

George decided that he would not accept Elizabeth's request to be set free via a letter, and stated that he would only believe it when he heard it from her own lips. On Thursday 21st August 1823, he set out on the long journey from Manchester to Wigwell Hall. He travelled by train first to Derby, where he stayed in a hotel overnight. The following day, he caught another train to Whatstandwell, where he booked a room in the Bull's Head.

After taking a pill with some brandy to calm his nerves, he set out on foot to walk the four miles to Wirksworth, calling at several hostelries on the way to fortify himself with a brandy in each. He also called on Revd Herbert Harris, the headmaster of Wirksworth Grammar School, a man he knew slightly. To Revd Harris, the 25-year-old George Townley seemed calm and collected. They discussed George's problem, and Revd Harris confirmed that Elizabeth Goodwin was now seeing a young clergyman, though he refused to give George his name.

When George Townley reached Wigwell Hall at 5.30pm, he was received courteously. As instructed by Elizabeth, the housekeeper, Mrs Poyser, admitted him to the house. Elizabeth came down to see him and the two went for a walk in the garden. After tea, Elizabeth met George again and they went for another walk, this time outside the grounds. When Elizabeth tried to say a final goodbye to him, George produced a large pocket knife and stabbed her three times in the neck.

He did not attempt to flee the scene, and even went over to the dying girl and kissed her. Elizabeth was carried back to Wigwell Hall. George Townley waited with her grandfather until a doctor and a police constable arrived. The doctor pronounced the girl dead, and Townley was arrested. To everyone who asked, Townley said that he had killed Elizabeth because she had proved false to him. To one he commented that he knew that he would be hanged for it. He did not seem mad or even angry at the time of his arrest.

He handed over the murder weapon to the police, and said that he felt much happier now that he had killed Elizabeth, adding callously that he hoped she was happier too. An inquest found that Elizabeth Goodwin had been wilfully murdered and named George Victor Townley as her killer.

Townley's trial took place in Derby on 11th December. None of the facts of the case were in dispute. The main matters for the jury to consider were whether the accused man had gone to Wigwell Hall with the intention of killing his former fiancée, and whether he was sane at the time of committing the deed. He denied that he had gone to see Elizabeth with murder in mind, but Mrs Poyser, the housekeeper, gave evidence that Elizabeth had told her that on his first talk with her, he had said that if she would not go away with him he would make sure she could not marry anyone else.

Everyone who gave evidence stated that George Townley had seemed perfectly rational in his manner on the day of the crime. He had understood what he had done, and had spoken of being hanged for it. The jury did not believe that he was insane and found him guilty of murder. The judge sentenced him to death.

However, he was not to be executed for his crime. An inquiry was held and he was interviewed about the murder. During the interview he stated that he did not feel that he was guilty of doing anything wrong. He argued that their engagement was the same as a marriage and it was perfectly in order for a man to kill a wife who had been unfaithful to him! He even stated, 'Bessie Goodwin was my property and I had a right to do what I did as she had proved false to me.'

Despite all of this, he was eventually found insane and sentenced to life imprisonment. He was first sent to the mental hospital for the criminally insane at Bedlam, and then to Pentonville prison. There he eventually killed himself by jumping off the chapel roof.

BIBLIOGRAPHY

Baggoley, Martin, *Derbyshire Murders*,
The History Press 2008

Bell, David, *Derbyshire Tales of Mystery and Murder*,
Countryside Books 2003

Eddlestone, John J., *Murderous Derbyshire*,
Breedon Books 1997

Garner, Edward, *Hanged for Three Pennies*,
Breedon Books 2000

Lomax, Scott C., *Deadly Derbyshire*,
Wharncliffe Books 2011

Lomax, Scott C., *Unsolved Murders In and Around
Derbyshire*, Wharncliffe Books 2009

Nutt, Graham, A Stranger, *A Ghost and A Conjuror*,
Avenger Publications 1996

Smith, Roly, *Murder and Mystery in the Peak*,
Halsgrove 2004